D0100238

in a nutshell

Advertising is the structured communication of information, generally intended to persuade individuals to purchase products or services. It is just one component of the marketing process. Advertising plays a key role in improving our standard of living in a free-market economy; however laws exist to keep the practice of advertising honest and ethical.

The following questions will test your take-away knowledge from this chapter. How many can you answer?

LO.1. Define advertising and distinguish it from other forms of marketing communications.

LO.2. Explain the role advertising plays in business and marketing.

LO.3. Illustrate the functions of advertising in a free-market economy.

LO.4. Discuss how advertising evolved with the history of commerce.

LO.5. Describe the impact of advertising on society.

Practical Application

LO.1.

• Television commercials, Web sites, text messages, coupons, telemarketing calls, and e-mails are just a few of the many marketing _____ tools that companies and organizations use to initiate and maintain contact with their customers.

• Albert Lasker defined advertising as _____ in print.

• In order to win converts to a product, service, or idea, advertising must be _____.

• Word-of-mouth advertising is not an advertising medium because it's not structured, openly sponsored, or _____.

LO.2.

• _____ is an organizational function and a set of processes for creating, communicating, and delivering value to customers.

• Developing products, pricing them strategically, distributing them so they are available to customers at appropriate places, and promoting them through sales and advertising activities constitutes the 4Ps of the _____.

• The ultimate goal of marketing is to earn a _____ for the firm.

• An effective advertising specialist must have a broad understanding of the whole _____ process in order to know what type of advertising to use in a given situation.

LO.3.

• _____ has driven the growth of advertising since its earliest beginnings.

• Access by buyers and sellers to complete information leads to greater _____ and lower prices for all.

• A(n) _____ exists when the sale or consumption of a product may benefit or harm other people who are not involved in the transaction and didn't pay for the product.

LO.4.

• Through product differentiation, many products become special not because of their ingredients but because of their _____.

• A product's unique selling proposition _____ it from competitive products.

• Advertisers use _____ to slow the demand for their products.

• Advertising creativity is not about winning awards, but about helping _____ things.

• To do a better job of relationship marketing, advertisers must _____ all their marketing communications with everything else they do.

LO.5.

• By publicizing the material, social, and cultural opportunities of a free enterprise society, advertising has encouraged increased _____ by both management and labor.

• The biggest opponents of unethical advertisers are advertisers who embrace _____ communication practices.

Did your answers include the following important points?

LO.1. Define advertising and distinguish it from other forms of marketing communications.

• Advertising is the structured and composed nonpersonal communication of information, usually paid for and usually persuasive in nature, about products by identified sponsors through various media.

• Non-advertising forms of marketing communications do not fit that definition in one or more ways. They may be unstructured conversations or not be paid for by a sponsor, such as word-of-mouth. Or they may be directed to just one individual, such as personal selling.

LO.2. Explain the role advertising plays in business and marketing.

• Marketing is a business function that creates, communicates, and delivers value to customers, and advertising helps business achieve its marketing goals.

• Advertising does this by refining the target audience and informing, persuading, and reminding that audience about the need-satisfying value of the company's goods and services.

LO.3. Illustrate the functions of advertising in a free-market economy.

• Identify products and differentiate them from others by developing strong brand names and creating unique graphics and packaging.

• Communicate information about the product, its features, and its place of sale by announcing its benefits, its price, and where it is sold.

• Induce consumers to try new products and to suggest reuse by offering trial samples, distributing coupons to encourage purchase, and providing in-store displays.

• Stimulate the distribution of a product by providing incentives for retailers to stock it.

• Increase product use by making consumers feel good about consuming it.

• Build brand value, brand preference, and loyalty by running competitive advertising campaigns.

• Lower the overall cost of sales by efficiently delivering the above messages to millions of consumers through mass media.

LO.4. Discuss how advertising evolved with the history of commerce.

• Thousands of years ago, there was no need for advertising because products were made in small quantities and people lived close together.

• Over time, the growth in population, the increase in productivity, improvements in transportation, advances in technology and education, the growth in affluence, and the rise of competition created both the need and the opportunity for advertising to fuel commerce.

• Today, digital technology is reshaping the ways customers will receive and interact with advertising.

LO.5. Describe the impact of advertising on society.

• Advertising has improved our standard of living by helping consumers match products to their needs, supporting the media, and promoting important social issues and causes.

• But advertising has also gone through periods during which it struggled with honesty and ethics.

chapter two

active review card
The Economic, Social, and Regulatory Aspects of Advertising

in a nutshell

Advertising is both applauded and criticized for the role it plays in selling products and influencing society. Critics say advertising is deceptive and makes our society too materialistic. Proponents argue that advertising stimulates healthy competition and raises the overall standard of living. Government agencies, organizations, the media, and the advertising industry itself regulate advertising to minimize the negative effects.

The following questions will test your take-away knowledge from this chapter. How many can you answer?

LO.1. Describe the impact of advertising on the economy.

LO.2. Examine the validity of the various social criticisms of advertising.

LO.3. Explain the difference between social responsibility and ethics in advertising.

LO.4. Describe how government agencies regulate advertising to protect both consumers and competitors.

LO.5. Discuss the activities of nongovernment organizations in fighting fraudulent and deceptive advertising.

Did your answers include the following important points?

LO.1. Describe the impact of advertising on the economy.

- Advertising contributes to the number of sellers, which increases competition and gives buyers more choices.
- Advertising enables manufacturers to engage in mass production, which in turn lowers the cost of products. These savings can then be passed on to consumers in the form of lower prices.
- Advertising keeps consumers informed of their alternatives and thereby allows companies to compete more effectively for consumer dollars.

LO.2. Examine the validity of the various social criticisms of advertising.

- Advertising is criticized for being deceptive. However, if a product does not live up to its ads, dissatisfaction occurs, something that is as harmful to the advertiser as to the buyer.
- Advertising is accused of manipulating us. However, you receive information from many different sources and ultimately act in your own self-interest.
- While the proliferation of advertising can be irritating, most people tolerate it as the price for free TV, freedom of the press, and a high standard of living.
- Advertisers have become more sensitive to stereotyping minorities and women. They are now usually portrayed favorably in ads because it's just good business.

LO.3. Explain the difference between social responsibility and ethics in advertising.

- Social responsibility means doing what society views as best for the welfare of people in general or for a specific community of people.
- Ethical advertising means doing what the advertiser and the advertiser's peers believe is morally right in a given situation.

LO.4. Describe how government agencies regulate advertising to protect both consumers and competitors.

- The Council of Better Business Bureaus monitors children's advertising for misleading or inaccurate content.
- The Federal Trade Commission (FTC) monitors Internet companies for violations of privacy policies. The FTC also regulates deceptive or unfair advertising.
- The Food & Drug Administration requires manufacturers to disclose all ingredients on product labels, in in-store product advertising, and in product literature. It regulates price promotions, the wording on packages, and nutritional labeling.
- The Federal Communications Commission (FCC) can restrict both the products advertised and the content of ads. The FCC also acts as an arbiter of broadcast decency and has the authority to license broadcasters (or take away their licenses).
- The Patent and Trademark Office and the Library of Congress protect trademarks and copyrights.

LO.5. Discuss the activities of nongovernment organizations in fighting fraudulent and deceptive advertising.

- The Better Business Bureau (BBB) protects consumers against fraudulent and deceptive advertising and sales practices.
- The National Advertising Review Council (NARC) promotes and enforces standards of truth, accuracy, taste, morality, and social responsibility in advertising.
- Almost all media companies review ads and reject material they regard as objectionable, even if it isn't deceptive.
- Consumer advocate groups investigate advertising complaints received from the public.
- The American Advertising Federation (AAF) defines standards for truthful and responsible advertising.

Practical Application

LO.1.

- Some people prefer branded products over unbranded products because advertising has given the brands added _____.
- In most product categories, the amount spent on advertising is _____ compared with the total cost of the product.
- The freedom to advertise encourages _____ sellers to enter the market.

LO.2.

- _____ refers to exaggerated, often subjective claims that can't necessarily be proven true or false.
- Advertisers themselves worry about the negative impact of excessive advertising, known as _____.
- Some advertising _____ all elderly people as weak and frail.

LO.3.

- Advertising that disturbs an advertiser's conscience is probably not _____.
- Providing *pro bono* (free) work to charitable organizations is an example of _____ responsibility.

LO.4.

- In 1982, the Supreme Court upheld an FTC order allowing physicians and dentists to _____.
- Internet users worrying about people they don't know getting personal information about them is a _____ issue.
- An ad is _____ if it contains a misrepresentation, omission, or any other practice that can mislead a significant number of reasonable consumers.
- An advertiser must be able to _____ any scientific claims it makes in its advertising.
- The _____ was responsible for determining if Janet Jackson's wardrobe malfunction during the 2004 Super Bowl was obscene.
- A _____ is any word, name, symbol, or device used by a manufacturer to identify his goods and distinguish them from those manufactured by others.

LO.5.

- A television commercial can be _____ by the broadcast standards department if it violates a network's policies.
- Newspaper ads that might easily be mistaken for regular reading material must feature the word _____

in a nutshell

There are many groups that work in the advertising industry. Within the group known as advertisers, different approaches characterize activities performed at the local, national, and international levels. Advertisers are assisted in developing campaigns by advertising agencies, which also come in many different forms. A broad range of tasks are performed by individuals within both independent ad agencies and in-house departments. In recent years, the commission system has become a less common way for agencies to be compensated for their work.

The following questions will test your take-away knowledge from this chapter. How many can you answer?

LO.1. List the various groups in the advertising business and explain their relationship to one another.

LO.2. Discuss the differences between local, national, and transnational advertisers.

LO.3. Explain how advertisers organize themselves to manage their advertising both here and abroad.

LO.4. Define the main types of advertising agencies.

LO.5. Explain the range of tasks people perform in an ad agency and an in-house advertising department.

LO.6. Discuss how agencies get new clients and how they make money.

Did your answers include the following important points?

LO.1. List the various groups in the advertising business and explain their relationship to one another.

- Advertisers are companies that pay to advertise themselves and their products.
- Advertising agencies help advertisers plan, create, and prepare IMC campaigns.
- Suppliers provide services that assist advertisers and agencies.

LO.2. Discuss the differences between local, national, and transnational advertisers.

- Local advertisers focus in a relatively restricted area.
- Local advertising includes product, institutional, and classified ads.
- National advertisers have a broad geographic reach. Their budgets are generally much larger than those of local advertisers.
- National and local advertisers differ in their focus, whether they plan strategically or tactically, time orientation, and whether they are made up of specialists or generalists.

LO.3. Explain how advertisers organize themselves to manage their advertising both here and abroad.

- Transnational advertisers deal with markets possessing different value systems, environments, and languages.
- Global marketers assume that product uses and needs are universal.

- National and multinational advertisers organize using a centralized or decentralized structure.

LO.4. Define the main types of advertising agencies.

- Agencies differ in their scope, range of services, and degree of specialization.

LO.5. Explain the range of tasks people perform in an ad agency and an in-house advertising department.

- Account executives are the liaison between the agency and the client.
- Research and account planning provide agency intelligence.
- Media planning and buying concerns selecting media time and space.
- Creative people, such as copywriters, art directors, and creative directors, plan and create the ads.

LO.6. Discuss how agencies get new clients and how they make money.

- Agencies get clients through referrals, presentations, and promotional activities.
- Agencies can be compensated in several ways. These include commissions, markups, and fees.
- The incentive (or pay-for-performance) system ties agency compensation to the campaign's effectiveness.

Practical Application

LO.1.

- Sandra decided that advertising could help her increase sales for her consignment shop. This makes Sandra a _____. Since Sandra knew relatively little about how to advertise effectively, she decided to work with an _____, an independent organization that plans, creates, and places advertisements.
- Benny works at a small ad agency. Benny often works with _____ who provide services such as video production, print production, and Web development. Most of the clients that Benny works with place ads in local _____, including radio and newspapers.

LO.2.

- There are three main types of local ads. _____ is designed to stimulate a sale of merchandise or to increase store traffic. On the other hand, _____ is intended to create a favorable perception of the business as a whole.
- Kendra's fast-food business is doing well, and she needs to hire five new cashiers. An inexpensive and effective way to do this is to use _____.

LO.3.

- When Tim started his business 20 years ago, he had only one brand, a shampoo. However his company now has five brands. Because Tim wants to maintain a high level of control across brands and take advantage of continuity and efficiency across divisional boundaries, he is organizing his ad department using a _____ organization.
- Mary has plans to sell her products in dozens of countries around the world. She assumes that the needs her products satisfy are universal, suggesting she intends to be a _____ marketer.

LO.4.

- Agencies that provide both advertising and nonadvertising services in all areas of communications and promotion are called _____ ad agencies.
- Kaitlin's company sells cash registers to large grocery chains. When she called a local consumer agency to see if it would represent her company, they directed her to a _____, since they are better equipped to represent clients that market to other businesses.

LO.5.

- Ed is interested in an update from his company's ad agency on the status of a campaign. He places a call to an _____ at the agency so he can get the information.
- Maria is a top copywriter with her ad agency. Naturally, she always works with her partner Stan, who is an _____. Stan and Maria's boss is a _____.
- Kelsie is an experienced _____ who figures out where ads should run. She supervises Greg, a _____, who contacts media companies and negotiates favorable rates.

LO.6.

- Brianna's agency insists that clients pay the standard 15 percent commission to her agency for its work. A client decides that it wants to buy $10,000 worth of advertising. This means that Brianna's agency will receive $_____ after making the buy.
- Marcus's agency lands a new client who insists that any compensation will depend on how the agency succeeds in increasing sales This is a form of compensation known as the _____.

chapter four

in a nutshell

Market segmentation is the process of identifying groups of people with similar characteristics who are likely to share an interest in your product. A target market can then be selected from these segments. A marketing mix comprised of the four Ps—product, price, place, and promotion—is designed to appeal to that target. The marketer fine tunes activities within those elements to maximize sales.

The following questions will test your take-away knowledge from this chapter. How many can you answer?

LO.1. Explain the role of advertising in facilitating satisfying exchanges.

LO.2. Illustrate the various methods advertisers use to segment and aggregate consumer and business markets.

LO.3. Discuss how defining a target market enhances a product's marketing strategy.

LO.4. Describe the elements of the marketing mix and the role advertising plays in each element of the mix.

Did your answers include the following important points?

LO.1. Explain the role of advertising in facilitating satisfying exchanges.

- One of the primary roles of advertising is to communicate a product's utility—the features and benefits that satisfy consumer needs and wants.
- Advertising also makes people aware of the availability of products, brand alternatives, price options, and where the products can be found. In the case of direct marketing, advertising may even close the sale.
- Finally, advertising reinforces satisfaction by reminding customers why they bought the product.

LO.2. Illustrate the various methods advertisers use to segment and aggregate consumer and business markets.

- **Behavioral** segmentation examines user brand loyalty, usage rates, purchase occasions, and benefits sought.
- **Geographic** segmentation looks at where users live, but also characteristics of where they live, such as weather, terrain, and population density.
- **Demographic** segmentation is based on statistical characteristics such as sex, age, ethnicity, education, occupation, and income.
- **Psychographic** segmentation groups people by their values, attitudes, personality, and lifestyle.
- Segmenting business markets is similar to segmenting consumer markets, but additional consideration must be given to the decision making process, type of industry, and customer size.
- Aggregating segments involves selecting groups that have a mutual interest in the product's utility and then combining them into larger market segments based on their potential for sales and profit.

LO.3. Discuss how defining a target market enhances a product's marketing strategy.

- The target market is comprised of those consumer segments that offer the greatest profit potential.
- Once a company defines its target market, it knows exactly where to focus its attention and resources.
- Marketers can then create a marketing mix (4Ps) fine-tuned to appeal to its target market.

LO.4. Describe the elements of the marketing mix and the role advertising plays in each element of the mix.

- **Product** is the way the product is designed, branded, and packaged and where it falls in its product life cycle. This information helps the advertiser competitively position the product, identify its points of differentiation, and determine which promotion strategies and tactics are most appropriate.
- **Price** influences consumer perception of a product and a brand's advertising must be consistent with its pricing strategy.
- **Place** is the method of distribution. Whether a product is sold directly or indirectly by the manufacturer will determine how and where it is advertised. And the intensity of distribution will influence the creative strategy as well as the types of consumer and trade promotions.
- **Promotion** includes all marketing-related communications between the seller and the buyer. Advertising is often the major promotion component, but marketing communication tools also include personal selling, sales promotion, direct marketing, and public relations.

Practical Application

LO.1.

- How a company knows what products to produce, where to distribute them, and through what channels is the focus of _____.
- A marketer needs to understand a product's _____ to the customer in order to know if it will satisfy the customer's functional needs and symbolic wants.
- If customers are _____, they will repurchase and tell their friends, especially in this new age of social media.

LO.2.

- When we see an ad that doesn't appeal to us, it may be because we're not in the _____ audience for the product being advertised.
- Since _____ users are already brand loyal, they require the least amount of advertising and promotion. On the other hand, _____ users are brand switchers and should be a primary target for brand advertising.
- The fact that McDonald's primary target market is children is an example of _____ segmentation.
- Harley Davidson might use _____ segmentation to identify men who are motivated by self-expressive needs.
- By combining segments that are relatively _____ an advertiser can construct a large and potentially very profitable target market segment.

LO.3.

- A _____ market are those consumers that a company wishes to appeal to, design products for, and tailor its marketing activities toward.
- Once a company has identified its potential customer, it can design a marketing _____, specifying its product, price, place, and promotion strategies.

LO.4.

- During the _____ phase of any product, a company must educate customers, build dealer distribution, and advertise heavily to establish a position as a market leader.
- A _____ strategy involves encouraging distributors and dealers to stock, display, and advertise new products. In contrast, a _____ strategy requires creating consumer demand.
- By developing a unique _____ for the brand in the consumer's mind, the marketer helps the consumer remember the brand and what it stands for.
- Franchising is an example of a _____ marketing system that benefits franchisees by centralizing the marketing efforts.

active review card
Communication and Consumer Behavior

in a nutshell

Advertising communication is used to persuade consumers to behave in a certain way. The successful IMC practitioner must understand the unique role advertising plays in the communication process and the way consumers behave in response to advertising communications. Ideally, this understanding results in the creation of effective messages.

The following questions will test your take-away knowledge from this chapter. How many can you answer?

LO.1. Explain how advertising differs from the basic communication process.

LO.2. Outline the consumer perception process and explain why advertising people say "perception is everything."

LO.3. Explain how a consumer's level of involvement with a product influences the decision-making process and the advertising approach.

LO.4. Describe the fundamental motives behind consumer purchases.

LO.5. Discuss the various influences on consumer behavior.

Did your answers include the following important points?

LO.1. Explain how advertising differs from the basic communication process.

- The basic communication process involves a source sending a message that is encoded in a channel and sent to a receiver who decodes the message. Feedback completes the cycle.
- The source of an advertising message may be real or imaginary. The source concept in an ad campaign includes both the sponsoring organization and the spokesperson.
- Semiotics, the study of how humans represent ideas symbolically, helps us to understand how advertising messages are interpreted.
- The receiver of an advertising message is ordinarily the consumer.

LO.2. Outline the consumer perception process and explain why advertising people say "perception is everything."

- Perception is the personalized way we sense, interpret, and comprehend various stimuli.
- An advertising stimulus is filtered by each member of the target audience through a set of physiological and psychological screens. This filtering process determines how the consumer responds to the message.

LO.3. Explain how a consumer's level of involvement with a product influences the decision-making process and the advertising approach.

- A consumer's level of involvement with a message is an important determinant of the processes of both learning and persuasion.

- High involvement messages are ones that the consumer finds personally relevant.
- Under high involvement conditions, consumer persuasion is facilitated by strong message arguments. Under low involvement conditions, persuasion is facilitated by peripheral message elements.

LO.4. Describe the fundamental motives behind consumer purchases.

- Motivation refers to the underlying forces that contribute to our actions. Motives stem from needs (instinctive forces that impel action) and wants ("needs" that are learned during our lifetime).
- Maslow believed that humans have a hierarchy of needs.
- Ads appeal to motives by promising a benefit or reward (positively originated or transformational motives) or by promising to solve a problem (negatively originated or informational motives).

LO.5. Discuss the various influences on consumer behavior.

- In addition to the personal factors, interpersonal influences are also important determinants of behavior. These interpersonal influences include family, social class, reference groups, and opinion leaders.
- Cultural and subcultural influences are also important. Culture is the set of beliefs and ways of doing things that are shared by a social group. Subcultures are segments that share meanings that distinguish them from the overall culture.

Practical Application

LO.1.

- In the American Express campaign that features real-life actor Jerry Seinfeld and fictional character Superman, who or what is the message source? _____.
- Fernando is a media planner. In the human communication process, his primary focus is likely to be on the _____.
- Beth's decision that instant feedback about her campaign is crucial would likely lead her to prefer _____ for the campaign.

LO.2.

- Objects that can stimulate our senses can be thought of as _____

- Ken wants every customer's dining experience in his new restaurant to be remarkable, so he pays careful attention not only to the taste of each dish, but to how they look and smell. His restaurant also has comfortable chairs and tables, and beautiful jazz melodies play softly in the background. Ken is obviously very focused on his diners' _____

- Laura knows it is not a good idea to lie out in the sun without sunscreen. However she rarely attends to messages that warn her of the danger involved. Laura is engaged in _____.

LO.3.

- Gina decides that an ad campaign for a camera should feature billboards that show a popular celebrity. The billboards feature very little copy. Consumer learning, in this instance, probably happens via _____

- Jed is interested in convincing young people that smoking is unhealthy. He creates a poster with detailed information about the

health problems that many smokers face. Jed is taking advantage of the _____ route to persuasion.
- Derick is starting a new pizzeria. His ads end in the tagline: "When you think pizza, think Derick's!" Derick's ultimate purpose with this campaign is to make choosing his brand a _____ when people think about pizza.

LO.4.

- Kirstie finds herself humming the campaign jingle from Checkers ads that say, "You gotta eat!" When Kirstie learns of Maslow's Hierarchy of Needs, she realizes that Checkers is appealing to a _____ need.
- Ben reads two advertisements for different brands of men's suits. One ad uses the slogan, "You have to wear a suit, but you don't have to spend a lot of money on it." The other ad reads "To feel important, you need to look important." Ben realizes that the first brand is appealing to _____ motives while the second appeals to _____ motives.

LO.5.

- A school asks a local agency to do a pro bono campaign to discourage teen drinking. The campaign features popular students at the school who do not drink. This campaign is taking advantage of the social influence known _____.
- Prior to his recent bad publicity, Tiger Woods made a great deal of money endorsing golf-related products. This likely stemmed from consumer perceptions that he was _____.
- A major advertiser develops two versions of every campaign, one in English and the other in Spanish. This is because of the growing consumer power of the Hispanic _____.

active review card
Account Planning and Research

in a nutshell

The account planner in an ad agency assures that the advertising strategy and executions are relevant to the target audience. Marketing research helps managers identify target audience needs and assess the effectiveness of marketing programs. Advertising research evaluates advertising concepts and executions. The research process involves several steps and there are many techniques available to the researcher.

The following questions will test your take-away knowledge from this chapter. How many can you answer?

LO.1. Describe the role of account planners in advertising agencies.

LO.2. Discuss how research can help advertisers select target markets, media vehicles, and advertising messages.

LO.3. Explain the basic steps in the marketing research process.

LO.4. Explain the common methods used in qualitative and quantitative research.

LO.5. Evaluate the challenges of pretesting and posttesting advertising.

LO.6. Identify issues that can affect the accuracy and usability of quantitative research.

Did your answers include the following important points?

LO.1. Describe the role of account planners in advertising agencies.

- The account planner's primary role is to represent the consumer during the process of planning advertising, nurturing a relationship between the consumer and the brand.
- The account planner applies a research perspective to ensure that the advertising strategy and executions are relevant to the target audience.

LO.2. Discuss how research can help advertisers select target markets, media vehicles, and advertising messages.

- Research can be used to determine which customers are primary users of the product category and to understand their demographics, geographics, psychographics, and purchase behavior.
- Syndicated research is used to evaluate which media vehicles reach the target audience most effectively and efficiently.
- Research can be used to explore what the target audience needs and wants with regard to the brands and products advertised.
- Research can also be useful in evaluating the effectiveness of creative ideas and finished advertising.

LO.3. Explain the basic steps in the marketing research process.

- The first step is to analyze the situation that the product is in and define the problem that advertising is intended to solve.
- Step two is to conduct informal research to learn more about the market, the competition, and the business environment, and to better define the problem.
- The next step is to develop objectives for research needed to address any unanswered questions.
- With objectives in hand, the next step is to conduct formal research. This research may be qualitative or quantitative or a combination.

- The final step in the research process involves interpreting and reporting the data in a manner clear to the company's managers.

LO.4. Explain the common methods used in qualitative and quantitative research.

- Qualitative research elicits in-depth, open-ended responses rather than yes or no answers. Techniques include focus groups, in-depth interviews, and ethnographic studies.
- Quantitative research is used to gain reliable, hard statistics about specific market conditions or situations. Techniques include direct observation of consumer behavior, experiments in which a test group receives the stimulus being tested, and surveys.

LO.5. Evaluate the challenges of pretesting and posttesting advertising.

- Pretesting of advertising takes place in an artificial setting—not in the environment where the consumer will ultimately view the advertising. Respondents may take on the role of expert advertising critics, try to please the interviewer, seek to select the "best" ad, or simply refuse to admit that they can be influenced by advertising.
- Posttesting measures whether respondents noticed the advertising and what they remember, but that doesn't tell the researcher whether they actually intend to buy the product.

LO.6. Identify issues that can affect the accuracy and usability of quantitative research.

- The accuracy and usability of quantitative research is largely determined by the method used to select the respondents and how many respondents are included in the sample.
- It's also important to construct the research questions in such a way that the respondents clearly understand what is being asked and the researcher draws the correct conclusions from the responses.

Practical Application

LO.1.
- Jeff Goodby believes that everything an agency does should be geared toward getting into people's _____ to figure out what they currently think and understand how best to influence them.
- Stanley Pollitt described _____ as the architects and guardians of their clients' brands, the detectives who uncovered long-hidden clues in the data and gently coerced consumers into revealing their inner secrets.

LO.2.
- Research can help managers assess the _____ of marketing programs and promotional activities.
- Advertisers can avoid mistakes and save money on production by _____ testing advertising ideas before they are finalized.

LO.3.
- Marketers can waste a lot of time and effort conducting research if they don't start by clearly defining the _____.
- Information previously collected or published, usually for some other purpose, by the firm or by some other organization is referred to as _____ data.

LO.4.
- Advertising researchers use _____ techniques to understand people's underlying or subconscious feelings, attitudes, interests, opinions, needs, and motives.
- In conducting a _____ market, marketers go to an isolated geographic area and introduce a product or test a new ad campaign or promotion before they roll it out nationally.

LO.5.
- Advertisers use _____ tests to determine how effectively their commercials perform in an environment surrounded by other commercials.
- Posttesting can measure whether a consumer will remember the advertising and even whether the advertising favorably influenced the respondent's attitude, but testing cannot accurately predict whether the consumer will actually _____ the product.

LO.6.
- Researchers need to select a _____ from the population, because they cannot survey everybody.
- Advertising researchers often use _____ samples because they're convenient to implement and provide sufficient accuracy for most ad testing.
- Research is considered _____ if it produces approximately the same result each time it is administered.

in a nutshell

Great advertising starts with effective planning. The planning process involves a careful analysis of the present situation, realistic setting of objectives, a set of strategies for achieving the objectives, and careful budgeting. Organizations generally develop a marketing plan before laying out the specifics of an IMC or advertising plan.

The following questions will test your take-away knowledge from this chapter. How many can you answer?

LO.1. Explain the role and importance of a marketing plan.

LO.2. Explain the difference between objectives, strategies, and tactics in marketing and advertising plans.

LO.3. Define what makes IMC planning different from traditional methods.

LO.4. Explain how to establish specific, realistic, and measurable advertising objectives.

LO.5. Explain how advertising budgets are determined.

Did your answers include the following important points?

LO.1. Explain the role and importance of a marketing plan.

- Marketing drives a company's income, so the marketing plan may be a company's most important document.
- The marketing plan assembles all relevant facts about an organization and lists goals and objectives for success.
- The marketing plan influences almost every decision about IMC and advertising.

LO.2. Explain the difference between objectives, strategies, and tactics in marketing and advertising plans.

- In top-down marketing, a company's plan has four elements: a situation analysis, marketing objectives, marketing strategies, and marketing tactics.
- An advertising or IMC plan extends the marketing plan's situation analysis to develop IMC objectives, IMC strategies, and IMC tactics.
- Marketing plan objectives are specific, realistic goals to be achieved in a specific period of time. They can be divided into need satisfying objectives and sales-target objectives.
- Marketing strategy describes how the company will meet its marketing objectives.
- Marketing tactics are the activities that will be executed.

LO.3. Define what makes IMC planning different from traditional methods.

- IMC is the process of building and reinforcing mutually profitable relationships by coordinating a strategic communications program through a variety of media or other contacts.

- IMC is guided by the assumption that everything a company does (and doesn't do) sends a message.
- IMC also encourages companies to gather a wealth of information about target markets in a database.

LO.4. Explain how to establish specific, realistic, and measurable advertising objectives.

- Setting realistic objectives requires an understanding of what advertising can do.
- The advertising pyramid offers one guide to setting objectives. It specifies a sequence of objectives that advertising should strive to achieve.
- Advertising objectives should be time-specific and quantified.

LO.5. Explain how advertising budgets are determined.

- In the percentage-of-sales method, the advertising budget is set as a fixed percentage of the prior year's sales of a good or service.
- The share-of-market/share-of-voice method links advertising dollars with sales objectives. If a company wishes to grow to a 20 percent share of market, it will need to spend enough money to achieve at least 20 percent share-of-voice (sponsor 20 percent or more of the IMC messages that the target audience receives).
- The objective/task method considers advertising a marketing tool for generating sales. After defining objectives and determining strategy, the objective/task method establishes a budget based on the estimated costs of achieving the objectives.

Practical Application

LO.1.

- Bill starts the new year wanting to find a way to increase sales of his product lines. If he were guided by a top-down perspective, the best way to begin would be to develop a _____.
- A typical marketing plan starts with a description of the brand and company's current circumstances. This section is known as the _____.
- In a SWOT analysis, the difference between strengths and weaknesses on the one hand, and opportunities and threats on the other, is that the former are _____ to the company while the latter are _____.

LO.2.

- Ray owns a small store. To increase sales, he decides to put everything on sale at half price. Ray's sale is an example of a marketing _____.
- Claire owns another store. She does well selling her products to young women, but thinks she can increase profits by also selling to young men. To attract this new target audience she will need a marketing _____. Claire decides that in the next quarter she will increase sales to young men by 25 percent, an example of a marketing _____.

LO.3.

- Tameka is a consultant to small firms. Since she has embraced the IMC perspective, she finds herself constantly reminding these firms to focus less exclusively on sales and more on _____.

- Karen's company sells jewelry. Her ad manager, Ellen, suggests that they reconsider one of their suppliers because of concerns over child labor. Karen doesn't see that it matters who she buys from, but Ellen reminds her that even _____ messages can impact consumer attitudes.

LO.4.

- Ken decides that advertising will increase sales of his products by 20 percent. Elena reminds him that good objectives are not just quantifiable; they also include a _____ element.
- John hopes to use the advertising pyramid to write his advertising objectives. Since his product is brand new and largely unknown in the marketplace, he realizes that his initial objectives should focus on _____ and _____.
- Brianna thinks that consumers buy her product more on the basis of impulse and emotion, not the thoughtful, rational process of the advertising pyramid. She is convinced that sales will go up if she moves her product close to the register where customers can see it easily. If so, her consumers are less likely to follow a learn-feel-do model, and more likely to follow a _____ model.

LO.5.

- Ed uses the percentage-of-sales method to set his advertising budget. Last year his sales decreased, so this year he will spend _____ on advertising.
- Jenny uses the share-of-voice method for budgeting. Her sales are down but her competitors are spending more on advertising. If she continues using share-of-voice, Jenny will spend _____ on advertising this year.

in a nutshell

In this chapter you will learn how advertising strategies, the subject of Chapter seven, lead to the development of creative and message strategies that guide the creative process. At the heart of great advertising is creativity. The creative team must not only generate great ideas, it must avoid common pitfalls that derail fresh and innovative approaches.

The following questions will test your take-away knowledge from this chapter. How many can you answer?

LO.1. Identify the members of the creative team and their primary responsibilities.

LO.2. Describe the qualities of great advertising.

LO.3. Explain the role of the creative strategy and its principal elements.

LO.4. Discuss ways that creativity enhances advertising.

LO.5. Define the four roles people play at different stages of the creative process.

Did your answers include the following important points?

LO.1. Identify the members of the creative team and their primary responsibilities.

- Copywriters develop the verbal message.
- Art directors develop the nonverbal aspects of the message, those elements that determine the look and feel of the ad.
- The creative team works for a creative director, the person who is ultimately responsible for the creative product.

LO.2. Describe the qualities of great advertising.

- Great ads have two important qualities: audience resonance and strategic relevance.
- To resonate means to echo or reverberate. Ads that resonate have the "boom" factor, the surprise element that stops the audience in its tracks.
- The relevance factor links the ad to the sponsor's strategy. Ads must do more than entertain, they must elicit the desired action, feeling, or beliefs toward the brand.

LO.3. Explain the role of the creative strategy and its principal elements.

- The creative strategy is a simple written statement of the most important issues to consider in developing an ad.
- A creative strategy ordinarily describes the problem the advertising must solve, the advertising objective, a benefit statement, a support statement, the brand's personality, and special requirements.

- Delivery of the creative strategy marks the beginning of message strategy development.

LO.4. Discuss ways that creativity enhances advertising.

- Creativity is the act of combining two or more previously unconnected objects or ideas into something new.
- Creativity enhances advertising by helping to inform, persuade, and remind. Creativity puts the "boom" in advertising.

LO.5. Define the four roles people play at different stages of the creative process.

- The creative process can be defined by the roles that the creative team plays during ad development.
- The explorer role involves a search for new information, with special attention to unusual patterns.
- The artist role involves experimentation and playing with different approaches in the search for an original idea.
- The judge role involves evaluating different options and choosing the most practical one.
- The warrior role involves overcoming the personal and social obstacles to bringing a creative concept to realization.

Practical Application

LO.1.

- Jorge believes his skills and interests best suit doing advertising layout and design. A good job inside an agency for Jorge would be _____.
- Regina and Donna are the creative team on an account. After they finish brainstorming, they are looking forward to presenting their ideas to their boss, _____.

LO.2.

- Rodney's creative director discusses a problem that he has with one of Rodney's ads. The ad is very entertaining and creative, says the CD. However it does not convey the brand's benefit very clearly. The creative director is saying the ad does pretty well on the _____ dimension but poorly on the _____ dimension.

LO.3.

- Lauren and Chris are a creative team and are anxious to get started on their new client's ads. But before any ads can be developed, they need a roadmap. The document that serves as this roadmap is the _____.
- Nick is working on his first creative strategy and is not sure where he should start. His creative director suggests that Nick begin by stating the _____.
- Zora believes that the women in her brand's target audience will be more attracted to it if it is seen as sophisticated and beautiful.

She makes sure to tell her creative team that these elements need to be noted in the part of the creative strategy that deals with the _____.

LO.4.

- Colin is working on a bicycle helmet account. He knows that most parents know the value of encouraging their children to wear a helmet. He also knows they often forget to make sure that their child wears one. He decides that the primary purpose of creativity in his ads should be to _____.
- Jim works on the account for a brand of oatmeal. He has examined research that suggests that oatmeal can help some people reduce their cholesterol. He also knows that very few people in his target audience are aware of the research. He decides that the primary purpose of creativity in his ads should be to _____.

LO.5.

- When Sarah asks her creative team to toss out ideas, no matter how wild and crazy, and not worry about their practicality, she is playing the role of the _____.
- Devon and Marcus are proud of a campaign idea they've come up with, but they know they will face resistance from the client, who is very cautious. They meet for several hours to review every possible objection the client might offer. During the meeting, the client does in fact seem dubious about their ideas, but the team finally wins him over. They have been playing the role of the _____.

in a nutshell

The creative team can include a variety of specialists who conceptualize, design, write, and produce IMC materials. To be successful, these individuals must know the copywriting and commercial design terms and formats. They must also possess an aesthetic sensitivity so they can recognize, create, evaluate, or recommend quality work.

The following questions will test your take-away knowledge from this chapter. How many can you answer?

LO.1. Describe the factors involved in creating print ads.

LO.2. Explain the types of copy and how great copy is created in print ads.

LO.3. Outline how great copy is created in electronic ads.

LO.4. Discuss the role of art in electronic ads.

LO.5. Review the unique requirements in writing for the Web.

Did your answers include the following important points?

LO.1. Describe the factors involved in creating print ads.

- Design refers to how the designer chooses and structures the artistic elements of an ad.
- A layout is an overall orderly arrangement of all the format elements of an ad.
- The design process is both a creative and an approval process. Thumbnails, roughs, dummies, and comps are used to establish the ad's look and feel. The approval process takes place each step of the way.

LO.2. Explain the types of copy and how great copy is created in print ads.

- The advertiser tells the complete sales story in the body copy, or text.
- Common copy styles include straight sell, institutional, narrative, dialogue/monologue, picture caption, and device.
- The keys to good body copy are simplicity, order, credibility, and clarity. The four basic format elements used for long copy are the lead-in paragraph, interior paragraphs, trial close, and close.

LO.3. Outline how great copy is created in electronic ads.

- Radio copy begins with a script, which resembles a two-column list, with sound effects on the left and dialogue on the right.

- To get attention, the ad message must be catchy and unforgettable. Radio listeners decide within a few seconds whether they will listen.
- Television copy also begins with a script, but the left side is titled "video" while the right is "audio."
- Broadcast commercials must be believable and relevant.

LO.4. Discuss the role of art in electronic ads.

- Creating the concept for radio or TV advertising is similar to concepting for print: the first step is determining the big idea.
- Formats for radio and TV commercials include straight announcements, presenter, testimonial, demonstration, musical slice of life, lifestyle, and animation.
- After the creative team selects the big idea and format, a script is developed. In the case of TV, a storyboard often follows.

LO.5. Review the unique requirements in writing for the Web.

- The designer should understand that the Internet is a completely new medium that engages users in a different way.
- Perhaps no consideration in design is more important than understanding why people visit a site in the first place. Visitors arrive with a purpose.

Practical Application

LO.1.

- Drew and Jody began thinking about the look and feel of the ad they were designing. Their thoughts focused on the _____, which is the orderly arrangement of the format elements.
- After Drew and Jody began their discussions, Jody was hit by an insight that she wanted to get down on paper. She prepared a quickly drawn 3" × 4" _____ to get a sense of what the ad might look like.
- Drew agreed that Jody's idea was a good one, so he suggested she sketch a _____, which is drawn to the actual size of the ad.

LO.2.

- Gerard thought very carefully about the words he would use in an ad's _____, since it contains the words that will be read first and are most likely to draw attention.
- When Donna, a creative director at an ad agency, looked over the headlines she received from her creative team, she knew something was missing. She sat them down in her office and asked what the headlines "When it absolutely, positively has to be there overnight" and "folds for easy storage" have in common. Her team knew the answer was that each offered readers an easy to grasp _____.
- John looked over a rough and suggested that his team move a key subheadline above the headline. He did so by pointing to the subhead and saying, "Make that one a _____."

LO.3.

- Jim scribbled a note to his partner to be a bit clearer about the SFX. His partner knew immediately that Jim was referring to the ad's _____.

- Paul began developing a script for a TV commercial. He quickly divided the script page into a space for _____ on the left side and _____ on the right.

LO.4.

- Linda knew the script for her TV commercial script would not suffice in showing her creative idea to the client. So she created a series of _____ that depicted the artistic approach, action sequences, and the style of the commercial.
- Glenda and Bob debated a broadcast commercial idea back and forth. Finally Glenda suggested that they use the oldest and simplest type of TV commercial, the _____. It would feature one person, an announcer, delivering the sales message.
- The Big Idea Ad Agency filmed dozens of actual consumers using its client's product using a hidden camera. Its goal was to use the positive consumer reviews in a _____ ad.

LO.5.

- Jen and Tim were brainstorming about the design of a new company Web site. Since Jen had experience with Web site design, she shared with Tim that no design consideration is more important than understanding _____.
- Nick reminded his client that the purpose of a banner ad is _____.
- Shamika knew her client had little money to spend on media but had a fantastic product. She decided that a video posted to YouTube that demonstrated the product's effectiveness would help her client achieve her marketing objectives. This type of ad, she explained to her client, is called a _____.

in a nutshell

In this chapter you will learn about how ads and commercials are produced for print, electronic, and digital media. With their dynamic effect on the production process, computers give advertisers more options for saving money and time. But to control costs and ensure quality, advertisers need a basic knowledge of the processes and methods used in printing and broadcasting as well as in the new digital media.

The following questions will test your take-away knowledge from this chapter. How many can you answer?

LO.1. Understand ways to save money in print and electronic production.

LO.2. Explain the processes for producing print ads and brochures.

LO.3. Explain the production process for radio ads.

LO.4. Describe the major production techniques for TV commercials.

LO.5. List ways that digital media save money as compared with print and electronic media.

Did your answers include the following important points?

LO.1. Understand ways to save money in print and electronic production.

- Five problems commonly break budgets: inadequate planning, production luxuries, overtime, special equipment, and a complex hierarchy of decision makers.
- In print, a big cost factor is the engraver. For collateral materials, the cost of paper is also important.
- In radio, the primary costs are associated with talent and music.
- Television costs, in addition to those associated with talent and music, vary as a function of the director, large casts, animation, special effects, use of multiple locations, and script changes.

LO.2. Explain the processes for producing print ads and brochures.

- Preproduction begins when the creative department submits the approved creative concepts to production.
- Art directors select the type styles to enhance the personality of the product, guided by readability, appropriateness, appearance, and emphasis.
- Planning the job involves choosing a color guide and a printing process. The production manager must decide whether to emphasize speed, quality, or economy.
- The production phase involves creating the visual, preparing mechanicals, and getting camera-ready art and halftones ready.
- The prepress phase involves stripping, preparing negatives, and creating plates.
- Finally, the duplication and distribution phase involves printing, binding, and shipping.

LO.3. Explain the production process for radio ads.

- The preproduction phase for creating radio commercials involves assigning a radio producer to hire a studio and director, choose the talent, estimate costs, and prepare a budget.
- Production is when the spot is cut.
- In postproduction the spot is edited and mixed. The final master tape is copied to create dubs.

LO.4. Describe the major production techniques for TV commercials.

- As with radio, production goes through three steps: preproduction, production, and postproduction.
- Preproduction includes selecting the right production technique from live action, animation, or special effects.
- Production is also called the shoot. Specialists help with sound, lighting, camera work, and directing the talent.
- In postproduction, film is edited and mixed. Editors have different choices depending on whether they have used video or film.

LO.5. List ways that digital media save money as compared with print and electronic media.

- Digital media give marketers new ways to reach prospects and begin a relationship.
- Production costs can be quite high for some digital media. But these costs are balanced by the low costs of delivering the message and the virtual absence of limitations on space or time.
- Compared with traditional media, digital advertisers can offer prospects more information at a lower price.

Practical Application

LO.1.
- Niles looks over the production costs of an ad campaign and finds they are too high. He needs to figure out why things got out of hand. His boss, Terry, suggests five areas that typically bust budgets in advertising. They include _____.
- Brittany realizes that she is far from exhausting her radio production budget. Two items worth considering that can easily use up her excess cash are _____ and _____.

LO.2.
- The creative department submits approved creative concepts to Devon, who opens a job jacket. This marks the official beginning of the _____ phase of the print ad.
- Sandra is confident that production costs for her ad will be low since it is only comprised of a single solid color. The artwork, she explains to her printer, is just _____.
- Bob drops off the mechanicals for an ad with the production department. Bob knows that mechanicals are _____ of the artwork.

LO.3.
- Esther and Joe disagree about which type of spot to use for their client. Joe wants to use a live commercial, but Esther counters that live commercials have two big disadvantages: _____ and _____.

- The talent for a commercial has been hired and the actors are rehearsing their dialogue. One individual seems to be supervising the actors and even suggesting ways they read their lines. This supervisor is most likely the commercial's _____.
- Greta is listening in as a radio spot is being recorded. She believes that one of the microphones is too loud in the studio, and asks the recording engineer to adjust it by using the _____.

LO.4.
- Naomi is creating a blueprint of her agency's TV commercial that features sketches of key scenes and dialogue. The technical term for Naomi's blueprint is _____.
- Tameka will have to be very careful with the _____ of the commercial, since this is the one that is copied to produce all of the dupes.

LO.5.
- Peter wants to convince his boss that a viral campaign can help the company save money. His boss asks whether the savings will come from the cost of producing the viral film. Peter says no, but that he does expect savings from the fact that it _____.

in a nutshell

Print media provide unique and flexible opportunities for advertising creativity; their messages last much longer than those in broadcast media. Print advertising includes magazines and newspapers, but it may also include any message that is produced on printed surfaces. All print advertising has several unique elements in common. Many factors must be considered by media buyers when evaluating print.

The following questions will test your take-away knowledge from this chapter. How many can you answer?

LO.1. Explain the advantages and disadvantages of magazine advertising.

LO.2. Discuss how magazine circulation is measured and rates are set.

LO.3. Explain the advantages and disadvantages of newspaper advertising.

LO.4. Describe the major types of newspapers and newspaper advertising.

LO.5. Discuss the various ways newspapers charge for advertising.

LO.6. Explain the unique roles played by directory and Yellow Pages advertising.

Did your answers include the following important points?

LO.1. Explain the advantages and disadvantages of magazine advertising.

- Magazines offer audience selectivity, high-quality color reproduction, creative flexibility, authority and believability, pass-along readership, long shelf life, and cost efficiency due to the selectivity.
- Drawbacks include lack of immediacy, limited reach per publication, high costs to reach mass audiences, long lead times, limited frequency, and significant clutter.

LO.2. Discuss how magazine circulation is measured and rates are set.

- Primary circulation represents the number of people who buy a publication, either by subscription or at the newsstand. Secondary (or pass-along) readership is an estimate of how many people read a single issue of a publication.
- The rate base is the circulation figure on which the publisher bases its rates and is generally equivalent to the guaranteed circulation.
- Premium rates may be charged for special features and discounts may be given for volume purchases.

LO.3. Explain the advantages and disadvantages of newspaper advertising.

- Newspapers offer short leadtimes, geographic selectivity, wide reach, reader attention, creative flexibility, and reasonable cost.
- Drawbacks include low quality production, limited demographic targeting, a short life span, and a lot of clutter.

LO.4. Describe the major types of newspapers and newspaper advertising.

- Newspapers may be daily, weekly, or Sunday; standard or tabloid; local or national; paid or free; general interest or targeted to specific interests or populations.
- Advertising options include display ads, advertorials, classified ads, public notices, preprinted inserts, or even stickers affixed to the front page.

LO.5. Discuss the various ways newspapers charge for advertising.

- Newspapers may charge different rates to local and national advertisers. A flat rate is a nondiscounted price. Open rates are for one-time insertions and contract rates offer discounts for volume insertions. ROP rates allow the newspaper to place your ad anywhere in the paper; a preferred position rate gives you more control.

LO.6. Explain the unique roles played by directory and Yellow Pages advertising.

- Directories serve as locators, buying guides, and mailing lists, but they also carry advertising aimed at specialized fields. Most businesses need to advertise in directories that are directed at their audiences.
- The Yellow Pages is by far the most frequently used directory. Advertising is sold on an annual basis. Yellow Pages are often the sole advertising medium for local businesses. Advertising in the Yellow Pages is very expensive, but many companies would no longer be in business without it.

Practical Application

LO.1.

- People can read a magazine ad at their leisure; they can pore over the details of a photograph; and they can study carefully the information presented in the copy. This makes it an ideal medium for _____ involvement products.
- An important benefit of magazines is that they offer _____ readership; many people may read the magazine after the initial purchaser.
- Since magazine audiences are so selective, it's difficult to achieve a high level of _____ without running ads in many different magazines.

LO.2.

- If a magazine does not deliver the guaranteed circulation to its advertisers, it must provide a _____.
- _____ readership is measured by multiplying the number of readers per copy by the primary circulation to determine how many people read a single issue of a publication.
- *Accounting Monthly* would be considered a _____ publication because it is read by accountants who work in a variety of different industries.

LO.3.

- Newspapers offer advertisers many advantages. One of the most important is _____; an ad can appear very quickly, sometimes in just one day, and newspapers are read almost immediately by readers who are actively seeking information.
- In contrast to magazines, newspapers have a very _____ life span.

LO.4.

- _____ newspapers have a higher cost per thousand, but they also have a longer lifespan and more readers per copy.
- Retailers often run newspaper ads through _____ advertising programs sponsored by the manufacturers whose products they sell.
- Newspapers often rely heavily on _____ ads for profitability. However, many of these ads have migrated to Web sites like Craigslist and Monster.com.

LO.5.

- When advertisers place an ad, they submit an _____ order to the newspaper stating the date on which the ad is to run, its size, the desired position, the rate, and the type of artwork accompanying the order.
- Advertisers examine _____ to make sure ads ran according to instructions: in the right section and page position.
- Many newspapers offer _____ so that advertisers can test the effectiveness of different ads. The advertiser runs two ads of identical size, but different content, for the same product on the same day in different press runs.

LO.6.

- Yellow Pages ads should tell people _____ to make the purchase, not why.
- Unlike traditional Yellow Pages, which are typically published annually, Internet versions can be _____ routinely.
- As with most advertising media, the _____ the Yellow Pages ad, the more attention it attracts.

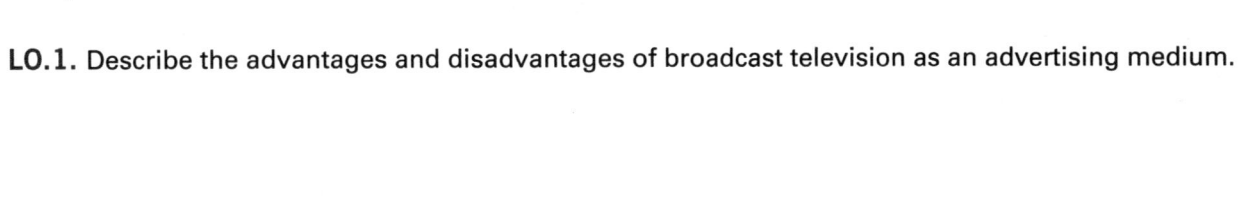

in a nutshell

Television is a powerful creative tool and offers advertisers a number of unique benefits as well as several drawbacks. Cable television is more targeted and has eroded broadcast TV's dominance. Due to zipping and zapping of TV commercials, in-show product placement is becoming more common. Radio also offers creative opportunities. TV and radio media buyers purchase the most efficient shows for their target audience.

The following questions will test your take-away knowledge from this chapter. How many can you answer?

LO.1. Describe the advantages and disadvantages of broadcast television as an advertising medium.

LO.2. Discuss the various options for advertising on television.

LO.3. Explain how to measure television audiences and select the best programs to buy.

LO.4. Describe the advantages and disadvantages of radio as an advertising medium.

LO.5. Explain the options for advertising on radio and how radio audiences are measured.

Did your answers include the following important points?

LO.1. Describe the advantages and disadvantages of broadcast television as an advertising medium.

- Television offers tremendous creative opportunities and has unmatched potential for viewer impact. It reaches a mass audience, at a relatively low cost per viewer, in a prestigious environment.
- On the downside, television advertising is very expensive, for production as well as for media time. It also takes a long time to produce and air TV commercials. Unless you are using cable television, it is difficult to target a specific audience. TV ads are very brief and air in an extremely cluttered environment, impacting recall. DVRs and remote controls make it very easy for viewers to skip commercials.

LO.2. Discuss the various options for advertising on television.

- Advertisers can purchase time on either broadcast or cable stations. Most network TV advertising is sold on a participation basis, though some advertisers will sponsor an entire program. Spot advertising runs between programs and can be geographically concentrated.
- There are also various syndicated program advertising opportunities, on reruns or original shows. Infomercials are program-length advertisements.
- Product placements within television shows are becoming increasingly popular as a tool to avoid viewers skipping advertisements.

LO.3. Explain how to measure television audiences and select the best programs to buy.

- Television audiences are measured by rating services which sample the viewing audience with meters and diaries. Ratings are reported within geographic markets (DMAs).
- A program's rating is the percent of television households in a specific market that are tuned to that specific program. GRPs tally the rating points achieved over a period of time (usually four weeks).
- Media buyers evaluate programs on the basis of cost per rating point (CPP) or cost per thousand people reached (CPM). Ideally,

they evaluate only the people reached who are in the advertiser's target audience.

LO.4. Describe the advantages and disadvantages of radio as an advertising medium.

- A lot of people listen to radio and they listen a lot. So radio can deliver reach and frequency very efficiently; both media and production costs are very reasonable. Since radio stations cater to specific audiences, advertisers can target their messages effectively. A well-written radio spot can be very engaging and can be tailored to the local market, even on short notice.
- Radio's biggest liability is the fact that it can be heard but not seen. This limits its effectiveness for some products. The narrowness of each station's audience also means that it's more difficult to saturate a market. Radio is also not always the focus of the listener's attention; it may not get noticed or an ad may get lost in the clutter of other ads.

LO.5. Explain the options for advertising on radio and how radio audiences are measured.

- Radio is generally purchased by format, based on the audience the advertiser is seeking. Satellite radio presents a relatively new alternative. National radio networks carry advertising to stations across the nation, while spot radio provides a choice of markets.
- Radio audience measurements have their own terminology. The average quarter-hour audience (AQH persons) is the number of people listening to a station for at least 5 minutes during an average quarter hour during a specific daypart The AQH rating is then the AQH persons divided by the population. Gross impressions are AQH persons times the number of spots. And GRPs are the gross impressions divided by the population.
- Cume persons is the number of *different* persons who tune to a radio station for at least five minutes during the course of a daypart. The cume rating is similar to the AQH rating, but unduplicated (like reach).

Practical Application

LO.1.

- Broadcast TV reaches its audience by transmitting signals through the air while _____ TV reaches its audience through wires or via satellite.
- Over half of adult viewers believe _____ is the most authoritative advertising source.
- Thanks to the _____ ability of cable TV, television can also be a highly selective niche medium.

LO.2.

- Most network TV advertising is sold on a _____ basis, with several advertisers buying 30- or 60-second segments within a program.
- A small advertiser with a small budget or limited distribution is likely to use _____ television advertising.
- People who watch a recorded show often skip through commercial messages, but by using _____, advertisers can minimize the impact of commercial avoidance.

LO.3.

- The benefit of _____ meters is that they go a step further than black boxes and gather information about who is watching in addition to the channel tuned.

- Some networks use elaborate schemes to improve their ratings during _____ periods, making the results not necessarily representative of the balance of the year.
- Television viewing is highest during the _____ daypart.
- The difference between audience share and rating is that _____ measures a show's audience as a percentage of only those televison sets that are turned on.

LO.4.

- The most common radio format is _____ music, which appeals to a broad cross section of Americans.
- The explosion of _____ will have the greatest impact on young listeners, who already listen to radio 20 percent less than the national average.

LO.5.

- Heaviest radio use occurs during _____ dayparts.
- If an advertiser orders radio spots on a run-of-station basis, the _____ determines in what dayparts the advertising will air.

in a nutshell

There are many important factors that advertisers must weigh when considering digital interactive media. Each medium has its own distinct characteristics and each has unique advantages and drawbacks. Advertisers must be able to compare the merits of these media and understand the most cost-effective ways to use them in their media mix.

The following questions will test your take-away knowledge from this chapter. How many can you answer?

LO.1. Discuss the various types of digital interactive media.

LO.2. Describe who uses the Internet and how they use it.

LO.3. Explain how time and space are bought on the Internet.

LO.4. Discuss the types of Internet advertising.

LO.5. Detail the problems with the Internet as an advertising medium and suggest ways to use it in IMC.

Did your answers include the following important points?

LO.1. Discuss the various types of digital interactive media.

- Digital interactive media include Web content such as Web sites, search engines, portals, and social media, DVD and Blue-ray catalogs and magazines, interactive TV, kiosks, and mobile advertising.

LO.2. Describe who uses the Internet and how they use it.

- The Internet has broad penetration in the United States, reaching nearly 75 percent of both men and women. Younger people tend to be somewhat more likely to use the Internet than older people. Wealthier and better-educated people are more likely to be Internet users when compared to poorer or less educated individuals.
- People use the Internet to upload photos, rate products, share files, create their own pages or blogs, and connect with others using social media.
- Software tools now allow advertisers to follow the online behaviors of millions of people.

LO.3. Explain how time and space on the Internet are bought.

- Media planners cannot think of the Internet in mass media terms because interactive media are personal audience venues. CPM, ratings, and share don't mean the same things in the interactive world.
- Advertising space on the Internet can be purchased in the form of banner ads, which are purchased on a CPM basis.

- Space in search engine results pages can be bought using keyword purchases. These are often priced by auctions and charges accrue to advertisers from click-throughs.

LO.4. Discuss the types of Internet advertising.

- Advertising on the Internet can be found in several venues. Web sites, microsites, and landing pages are popular locations for companies to communicate directly with consumers.
- Search engine giant Google has two programs, AdSense and AdWords, that place ads on Web sites and search engine results pages.
- Banners and their smaller cousins, buttons, continue to be a popular way of reaching Internet audiences.
- E-mail remains an inexpensive and effective way to target audiences for digital media.

LO.5. Detail the problems with the Internet as an advertising medium and suggest ways to use it in IMC.

- As with all media, the Internet has drawbacks. It is not a mass medium and may never offer mass-media effectiveness.
- As currently constituted, the many different forms of Internet advertising do not lend themselves to a single list of strengths and weaknesses. Smart advertisers will balance their Internet approaches.
- Advertisers who commit to social media for reaching audiences should be prepared to remain engaged.

Practical Application

LO.1.

- Unlike traditional media, which are centralized networks, the Internet is a _____ network.
- Many of the Web sites that attract the largest audiences each day are known as _____.
- The single most popular destination on the Web is _____, which reaches 40 percent of users each day.

LO.2.

- Terrence tells Mary that he doesn't want to use the Internet for an ad campaign because he believes women are not online as much as men. Mary responds that women's usage of the Internet, compared with men's, _____.
- Julia asks her friend Heather whether anyone really uploads photos to the Internet to share with others. Heather responds that this is a _____ activity for online users.
- In order to provide enhanced tracking, Web sites leave _____ on Internet users' computers.

LO.3.

- Banner ads on the Internet are generally priced on a _____ basis.
- Advertisers who are charged for click-throughs pay only when an Internet user arrives on the advertiser's _____.
- Contacting the millions of Internet sites and negotiating ad contracts would be nearly impossible for most advertisers. For this reason, most work through _____, which act as brokers.

LO.4.

- A _____ is used as a supplement to a Web site. For advertisers it is typically singular in focus and delivers on the current advertising message.
- The term used to describe a Web page that offers direct links to deeper areas of a Web site beyond the homepage is _____.
- _____ is Google's program that allows advertisers to bid on terms that deliver ads in the "Sponsored Links" area of a search results page.

LO.5.

- Tim is a social media consultant working with small business owner Alice. Alice asks Tim if he can just "put up a Facebook page for my company." Tim says that he can, but asks if Alice is committed to updating it daily. She says she is not, she just wants to be "on the Web." Will Alice likely be successful using this approach? _____.
- Gene and Roy disagree about digital media. Gene says that digital media cannot be all that important because companies spend less, in dollar terms, on digital than on traditional media. Roy says that is like comparing apples and oranges. What does Roy mean? _____.

chapter fourteen

in a nutshell

Media that reach people outside their homes is called out-of-home media. They include outdoor advertising, transit advertising, and less common alternatives like movie theaters and ATMs. Outdoor advertising is the least expensive medium per message delivered. Direct mail has always been one of the most effective media in terms of tangible results. Specialty advertising, used by many businesses, is very effective at improving the awareness and perception of a business.

The following questions will test your take-away knowledge from this chapter. How many can you answer?

LO.1. Discuss the various types of outdoor advertising and its pros and cons.

LO.2. Describe how outdoor advertising is purchased.

LO.3. Discuss the various types of transit advertising and its pros and cons.

LO.4. Discuss the various types of direct-mail advertising and its pros and cons.

LO.5. Describe the basic components of direct-mail advertising.

LO.6. Explain the value of advertising specialties.

Did your answers include the following important points?

LO.1. Discuss the various types of outdoor advertising and its pros and cons.

- Outdoor advertising is available in the very large bulletins, the common 30-sheet poster, and the urban 8-sheet (junior) poster. Digital billboards are becoming more common. Giant electronic spectaculars are found in some large cities.
- Outdoor advertising is visible 24/7 and cannot be turned off. It can reach a very large percentage of the population on a daily basis. It is a high-impact medium that can be targeted to specific geographic locations where the target audience is likely to see it. And it offers the lowest cost per exposure of any major medium.
- On the downside, outdoor is seen briefly, so the message must be short and impactful. It's also difficult to evaluate how many people actually notice outdoor advertising. The production cost can be quite high and the lead times very long.

LO.2. Describe how outdoor advertising is purchased.

- Outdoor has historically been purchased on the basis of a showing. A 100 showing means that the number of people that pass by the advertising in a day (the Daily Estimated Circulation) is equal to 100 percent of the market's population.
- A new measure—Eyes on Impressions—attempts to calculate the number of people that *actually* see the ad in a week.

LO.3. Discuss the various types of transit advertising and its pros and cons.

- Transit advertising targets people who use commercial transportation and includes bus and taxicab advertising as well as posters on transit shelters, terminals, and subways.
- Transit advertising gets frequent (daily) exposure for the extended period of time that people ride public transportation. As a result, readership is high and recall is excellent. The cost is very low and transit is an environmentally appropriate venue.

- The downsides include the obviously cluttered environment, the small space available, the potentially low status image, and an inability to target a selective audience.

LO.4. Discuss the various types of direct-mail advertising and its pros and cons.

- Direct mail can take the form of something as simple as sales letters or postcards to three-dimensional objects. E-mail is a relatively new form of direct mail. Also common are brochures, self-mailers, statement stuffers, house organs, and, of course, catalogs.
- The best thing about direct mail is the ability to be selective, down to a single person. There is tremendous creative opportunity, along with excellent production quality. Direct mail can be personalized and exclusive. Response rates are very high and fairly quick, making direct mail a good testing medium.
- However, direct mail is very expensive on cost per exposure. Mailing lists have errors and delivery times can be slow. Some people view direct mail as junk and immediately throw it away.

LO.5. Describe the basic components of direct-mail advertising.

- The mailing list is the heart of any direct-mail program. It defines the advertising's target market.
- The offer is the incentive or reward that motivates prospects to respond to a mailing, either with an order or with a request for more information. The offer must be clear and specific, it must promote a benefit to the recipient, and it must explain what the advertiser wants the recipient to do when he or she receives the mail.
- The creative package is developed by a creative team, just like other advertising. Production costs vary with the complexity of the mailer.

LO.6. Explain the value of advertising specialties.

- Advertising specialties are effective tools for improving people's perception and recollection of a business. Some specialty items are kept for years and serve as continuous, friendly reminders of the advertiser's business.

Practical Application

LO.1.
- Since customers pass quickly, outdoor advertising must be _____ to be effective.
- Outdoor advertising is priced at a very _____ cost per thousand impressions.

LO.2.
- The number of people who see outdoor advertising is largely a function of the outdoor board's _____.
- Due to concerns about _____, some cities have placed a moratorium on the construction of digital billboards.

LO.3.
- In transit advertising, a _____ showing means that one ad will appear in each vehicle in the transit system.
- _____ advertising describes the integration of advertising into the message delivery mechanism so effectively that the product is being promoted while the audience is being entertained.

LO.4.
- Consumers can _____ of receiving direct mail by contacting the Direct Marketing Association's Mail Preference Service.

- Some advertisers use business reply mail so the recipient can respond without paying _____.
- To keep down the cost of direct-mail advertising, many small advertisers participate in _____ mailings.

LO.5.
- Of the three basic components of direct-mail advertising, experts say the _____ is the most important.
- The advertiser's most important prospects will be found on the _____ list for direct-mail programs.
- The difference between a purchased and a rented mailing list is that a _____ list may be used for one mailing only.

LO.6.
- By far the largest product category for promotional specialty items is _____.
- _____ are promotional products that recipients typically must buy.
- An advertising specialty is a promotional product that's usually _____.

in a nutshell

There are many important factors that advertisers must weigh when considering digital interactive media. Each medium has its own distinct characteristics and each has unique advantages and drawbacks. Advertisers must be able to compare the merits of these media and understand the most cost-effective ways to use them in their media mix.

The following questions will test your take-away knowledge from this chapter. How many can you answer?

LO.1. Describe how media planning has changed over the past decades and what has caused these changes.

LO.2. Discuss the important types of media objectives and identify the terms that define strategies for achieving these objectives.

LO.3. Identify the factors that influence media strategy and tactics.

LO.4. Describe the different types of advertising schedules and the purpose for each.

LO.5. Explain the role of the media buyer.

Did your answers include the following important points?

LO.1. Describe how media planning has changed over the past decades and what has caused these changes.

- The purpose of media planning is to conceive, analyze, and creatively select channels of communication that will direct messages to the right people in the right place at the right time.
- Historically a relatively anonymous function, media planning began gaining prominence during the 2000s when clients began taking an a la carte approach to agency services.
- Several trends, including greater complexity of media options, increasing costs, and fragmented audiences, have made the media department's role even more important.

LO.2. Discuss the important types of media objectives and identify the terms that define strategies for achieving these objectives.

- Media objectives translate the advertising strategy into goals that media can accomplish. They have two major components: audience objectives and message-distribution objectives.
- Audience objectives define the types of people that the advertiser wishes to reach.
- Message-distribution objectives define where, when, and how often advertising should appear. Planners must understand key terms that include message weight, reach, frequency, and continuity to achieve message-distribution objectives.

LO.3. Identify the factors that influence media strategy and tactics.

- The factors that influence media strategy can be summarized as the five Ms: markets, money, media, mechanics, and methodology.

- Media strategy decisions are also influenced by the scope of the media plan, the sales potential of different markets, competitive strategies and budget considerations, media availability and economics, the nature of the medium and mood of the message, message size, length, and position considerations, and buyer purchase patterns.

LO.4. Describe different types of advertising schedules and the purpose for each.

- Selecting the right vehicle is an important tactic, and it is influenced by the campaign's objectives, the characteristics of audiences, and the exposure, attention, and motivation value and cost efficiency of media vehicles.
- Comparing exposure values of different vehicles can be difficult.
- The cost efficiency of different vehicles can be compared using CPM or CPP.
- Mixed media approaches provide synergy where the total effect is greater than the sum.
- Media can be scheduled to run either continuously or in a flighting or pulsing manner.

LO.5. Explain the role of the media buyer.

- The person in charge of negotiating and contracting with the media is called a media buyer.
- Some buyers specialize in different types of media.
- Successful media buyers have several key skills that include: knowing the marketplace, ability to negotiate, and monitoring performance.

Practical Application

LO.1.
- Jake is not sure he likes the quality of the media planning at his full-service agency. Fortunately for him, it is increasingly common for clients to go to _____ services for their media buys.
- Media objectives and strategies flow from the _____ plan.

LO.2.
- Beatrice, a media planner at a large agency, presents her thoughts for a media plan to her agency. She divides the presentation into two broad categories, _____ objectives, or who the advertiser wants to reach, and _____ objectives, or where and how often the message should appear.
- While newspapers are an example of a medium, the specific newspaper *The Wall Street Journal* is an example of a _____.
- Jamie is not sure that a local newspaper represents a good buy, pointing out that circulation figures are lower than the audience estimates of a local radio station. But Ann points out that circulation figures have to be multiplied by _____ to calculate the total audience.

LO.3.
- Scott wants to try to remember the factors that influence the media strategy, then he hears about the "5 Ms," which include _____, _____, media, mechanics, and methodology.
- Kyle wants to know the scope of a media plan for his agency's client. Dwight says it will be _____ because the advertiser has chosen a city to test-market the new product.

- Having introduced a new line of sunglasses, Dark Ray is looking for the right markets to buy advertising. Its agency is recommending Daytona, Florida, where lots of people wear sunglasses but not many people know about Dark Ray. It is, says an agency researcher, a classic case of a _____ BDI and a _____ CDI market.

LO.4.
- Dave looks over two magazines with similar readerships and compares their CPMs. Magazine 1 has a CPM of $25 while Magazine 2 is $17. If all else is equal, Dave will select Magazine _____.
- Sharon and Kayla are comparing CPMs for two TV shows. Kayla cautions Sharon that the CPM does not reflect the prevalence of the target audience for each show. Instead, says Kayla, they should look at the media statistic known as _____.
- Lisa's company does not have enough money to use a continuous schedule of media buys. She also knows that while her advertising should fluctuate, it should never disappear entirely. So she asks her agency to use a _____ schedule.

LO.5.
- Linda starts her first day on the job as a media buyer. Her boss Betty wants her to buy space in the local newspaper for a client. As Linda pulls out the newspaper's rate card, her boss indicates that the prices listed there are _____.

chapter sixteen

in a nutshell

The key to developing brand equity is to develop relationships with customers. To nurture those relationships, companies must integrate all of their marketing communications, with each other and with all other company functions. Direct marketing, personal selling, packaging, and sales promotion are some of the communications tools that must be integrated. Each tool serves a unique purpose; in combination they can create meaningful customer relationships.

The following questions will test your take-away knowledge from this chapter. How many can you answer?

LO.1. Explain the importance of relationship marketing and IMC.

LO.2. Discuss the benefits and challenges of direct marketing.

LO.3. Explain the various types of direct marketing activities.

LO.4. Describe the advantages and drawbacks of personal selling.

LO.5. Identify the elements that must be considered in establishing a trade show program.

LO.6. Explain the factors that must be considered in designing packaging.

LO.7. Describe the roles that sales promotion can play in a marketing strategy.

Did your answers include the following important points?

LO.1. Explain the importance of relationship marketing and IMC.

- The key to building brand equity in the 21st century is the development of interdependent, mutually satisfying relationships with customers and other stakeholders.
- Integrated marketing communications is the process of building and reinforcing relationships by developing and coordinating a strategic communications program through a variety of media or other contacts.

LO.2. Discuss the benefits and challenges of direct marketing.

- Direct marketing offers measurability, accountability, efficiency, and a high return on investment. The documentation of customer interactions in a database enhances the development of ongoing mutually beneficial relationships between marketers and customers.
- One challenge for direct marketing is that it suffers from the reputation created when direct marketers were hard-sell salesmen. Direct marketing also suffers from clutter, in the mail, on TV, and over the phone. Finally, many consumers are concerned with privacy and don't like that their names are in databases.

LO.3. Explain the various types of direct marketing activities.

- Personal direct selling is face-to-face sales outside a retail location.
- Telemarketing is direct selling over the phone, both outbound and inbound calls.
- Direct mail and catalog sales are types of direct marketing.
- Direct response print and television advertising can be very effective at stimulating customer responses.
- The Internet is already playing a major role in direct marketing and interactive television is likely to become a major vehicle in the future.

LO.4. Describe the advantages and drawbacks of personal selling.

- The greatest strength of personal selling is the sales rep's ability to interact face-to-face with the customer, gathering feedback, asking and answering questions, and demonstrating the product.
- The biggest liability of personal selling is its inefficiency; it is very time consuming and expensive.

LO.5. Identify the elements that must be considered in establishing a trade show program.

- Planning must consider the size and location of the space; the desired image of the exhibit; shipping, installing, and dismantling; the products to be displayed; storage and distribution of literature; preshow advertising and promotion; and costs.
- Budgeting must include the cost of the booth space and exhibits, travel, living, and salary expenses, and preshow promotion.
- The people staffing the booth must be articulate, people-oriented, enthusiastic, knowledgeable about the product, and empathetic listeners.
- A company's trade-show effort will not be productive if prospects' names are not collected and organized properly.

LO.6. Explain the factors that must be considered in designing packaging.

- Packaging must protect and preserve the product to reduce the effects of damage, pilferage, and spoilage, but in an environmentally safe way.
- Packages should use shape, color, size, interesting visuals, and even texture to deliver a promotional message.
- The package must inform customers of the product's features and benefits, while meeting government labeling requirements.

LO.7. Describe the roles that sales promotion can play in a marketing strategy.

- Sales promotion offers extra incentives to wholesalers, retailers, or customers to enhance or accelerate a product's sales movement.
- Sales promotions can be very effective in motivating customers to try a new brand or to select one brand over another.

Practical Application

LO.1.

- The key to building brand equity in the twenty-first century is the development of interdependent, mutually satisfying _____ with customers.
- Companies must integrate their marketing communications activities with all their other company functions so that all the messages the marketplace receives about the company are _____.

LO.2.

- Direct marketing is _____, meaning buyers and sellers can exchange information with each other directly.
- Because responses to direct marketing can be measured, direct marketing is _____.

LO.3.

- Good _____ can develop strong, lasting relationships with customers they have never met but with whom they speak every week.
- Advertising that asks the reader, viewer, or listener to provide feedback straight to the sender is called direct _____ advertising.

LO.4.

- The objective of personal selling should be to build a _____, a partnership that will provide long-term benefits to both buyer and seller.

- A superior salesperson is first and foremost a good _____.

LO.5.

- To stop traffic, a booth must be _____.
- The most common way customers learn about trade shows is through _____.

LO.6.

- The package is the last _____ a consumer sees before purchasing the product.
- If a marketer is planning to change a package design, it is advisable to make the change _____.

LO.7.

- While advertising helps develop and reinforce brand equity, sales promotion helps build short-term _____.
- _____ strategies, such as trade deals, are primarily designed to secure the cooperation of retailers.
- _____ is the most costly of all sales promotions but it is also one of the most effective for new products.

in a nutshell

Public relations is a process used to manage an organization's relationships with its various publics. A sponsorship is a fee paid to an organization in return for access to some commercial potential. Corporate advertising includes public relations advertising, institutional advertising, corporate identity advertising, and recruitment advertising. By integrating these tools with its general advertising activities, a company can improve the overall effectiveness of its marketing efforts.

The following questions will test your take-away knowledge from this chapter. How many can you answer?

LO.1. Distinguish between advertising and public relations.

LO.2. Describe the key tasks of public relations practitioners.

LO.3. Explain the potential benefits and drawbacks of sponsorships in an IMC plan.

LO.4. Discuss the functions of corporate advertising.

Did your answers include the following important points?

LO.1. Distinguish between advertising and public relations.

- Advertising reaches its audience through media the advertiser pays for. It appears just as the advertiser designed it, with the advertiser's bias built in. Knowing this, the public views ads with some skepticism or ignores them outright. Advertising is carefully placed to gain particular reach and frequency objectives.

- Many public relations communications are not openly sponsored or paid for. People receive these communications in the form of news articles, editorial interviews, or feature stories after the messages have been reviewed and edited by the media. Since the public thinks such messages are coming from the media rather than a company, it trusts them more readily. However, public relations objectives are not easy to quantify.

LO.2. Describe the key tasks of public relations practitioners.

- The PR practitioner analyzes the organization's relationships with its publics; evaluates people's attitudes and opinions toward the organization; assesses how company policies and actions relate to different publics; determines PR objectives and strategies; develops and implements a mix of PR activities, integrating them whenever possible with the firm's other communications; and solicits feedback to evaluate effectiveness.

- Specific tasks may include publicity and press agentry, crisis communications management, community involvement, public affairs and lobbying, speechwriting, fundraising and membership drives, publications, social media, and special-events management.

LO.3. Explain the potential benefits and drawbacks of sponsorships in an IMC plan.

- Sponsorships have the ability to involve customers, prospects, and other stakeholders. Marketers can select just those sponsorships that offer the closest fit with their target audience. Sponsorships can enhance a company's public image and provide face-to-face access to current and potential customers. And, depending on the venue, this access can be relatively uncluttered by competition. An added benefit is that sponsorships can boost the morale of employees and salespersons.

- Sponsorships can be very costly, especially when the event is solely sponsored. Co-sponsored events are more affordable, but they can be cluttered with many messages. Finally, evaluating the effectiveness of a particular sponsorship—separating the effects of a sponsorship from the effects of other concurrent marketing activities—can be challenging.

LO.4. Discuss the functions of corporate advertising.

- Public relations advertising may be used to improve the company's relations with labor, government, customers, suppliers, and even voters.

- Institutional advertising is aimed at enhancing a company's image with investors, employees, suppliers, or customers.

- Advocacy advertising is used to communicate a company's views on issues that affect its business, to promote its philosophy, or to make a political or social statement.

- Corporate identity advertising is used to reinforce a company's name, logos, or trademarks, especially when it merges with another company.

- Recruitment advertising is used to attract new employees.

Practical Application

LO.1.

- The primary role of public relations is to manage a company's _____.

- PR professionals refer to employees, customers, stockholders, competitors, suppliers, legislators, or the community as the organization's _____.

LO.2.

- A major activity of public relations, _____, is the generation of news about a person, product, or service that appears in print or electronic media.

- The tool used by PR professionals to publicize information is the _____ release.

LO.3.

- Yoplait's partnership with the Susan G. Komen Foundation, where Yoplait donated ten cents for each lid mailed in, is a good example of _____ marketing.

- One way to evaluate the effectiveness of sponsorships is to measure changes in _____ through pre- and post-sponsorship research surveys.

LO.4.

- An editorial that's paid for by an advertiser is referred to as a(n) _____.

- Many advertisers use _____ advertising campaigns to simultaneously communicate messages about their products and their company.